30 DAYS
TO FIND YOUR
PERFECT MATE

About the Author

Chuck Spezzano, PhD, is a world-renowned doctor of psychology, therapist, seminar leader, author, lecturer and visionary leader.

Over twenty-three years of counselling experience and nineteen years of advanced psychological research and seminar leadership, Chuck Spezzano created the breakthrough therapeutic healing model, the Psychology of Vision. The impact of the model has brought deep spiritual, emotional and material change to thousands of participants from Asia, Europe and North America.

Chuck Spezzano lives with his wife Lency and their two children, Christopher and J'aime, on the island of Oahu, Hawaii.

30 DAYS
TO FIND YOUR
PERFECT MATE

*The step-by-step guide to
happiness and fulfilment*

Chuck Spezzano, PhD

VERMILION
LONDON

Published in 1994 by Vermilion
an imprint of Ebury Press
Random House
20 Vauxhall Bridge Road
London SW1V 2SA

ISBN 0 09178982 6

Designed by Roger Walker

Typeset by SX Composing Limited, Raleigh, Essex
Printed and bound in Great Britain by
Cox & Wyman Ltd, Reading, Berkshire

Papers used by Ebury Press are natural, recyclable products
made from wood grown in sustainable forests.

*This book is dedicated with great thanks
to my wife and perfect mate, Lency*

Acknowledgements

Any book is truly a family project. After all, the family gives the writer to the world. I want to express gratitude for the loving support of my wife, Lency, who first edited the book, and our two children, Christopher and J'aime. I want to thank Peggy Chang for typing and general support, and editor Fred Perry – thank you both for adding your gifts to this work. I acknowledge A Course in Miracles for the seminal healing and teaching it has provided in my life, and I would further like to acknowledge my clients, workshop participants and past girlfriends who have given me so much and taught me so much over the years. These acknowledgements would be incomplete without my thanks to Sandi Mollod for her suggestions and support in getting this manuscript into print. My thanks go to Sam Westmacott for her intelligence, clarification and final editing of the work. And lastly, once again, thank you Lency, my wife, partner and true mate. Where would I be without you?

Introduction

This book is meant to be an exploration, an adventure.
When I first began work as a therapist, I was a staff psychologist at a drug rehabilitation centre. I discovered there was one thing more important to the participants in the rehabilitation programme than using drugs – learning vital healing information about themselves, their relationships, and their families.

In this book, there is a wealth of tried and accurate information, which has worked for thousands of people in my therapeutic practice and seminars over the last two decades. This exploration of your mind can save you pain, time and money, and, of course, assist you in finding your perfect mate.

To put it simply, the process in this book will work if you want it to. There are a number of exercises presented here which have, in and of themselves, manifested partners for people.

The thirty lessons work in two major ways: firstly to make room for a partner in your life, and secondly to invite in your perfect mate. The ideas may be strange and unnatural to your way of thinking at first; don't let that concern you, it's part of the process. You will learn and grow as you go along.

Trust your intuition. Whatever 'pops' into your mind is the easiest way, short of hypnosis, to bypass the well-defended, conscious mind. Whether you are aware of it or not, you are using your intuition all the time. Through your intuition, you see the world as you believe it to be. At the very least, your intuition presents the metaphoric truth, the symbolic patterns of your beliefs. But, if you are like most people, your mind will present the real truth as you know it. The mind at deeper levels is almost completely metaphoric, rather than literal; thus your intuition is a powerful and effective tool.

When you use your intuition it creates a natural flow of life-giving energy which is helpful to you and others.

The thinking mind and memory are tools, mere house guests, of your ego. They support the prevailing system of personality within you which is why your memory so conveniently supports the story of your life, but does not necessarily have anything to do with the ultimate truth (in which there would be no pain present), or even the relative truth (how things really happened objectively).

Get to know your intuitive mind; it will help to move you out of dissociative independence and into partnership or inter-dependence.

If answers to some of the questions in this book do not jump into your mind readily, then guess. That will have a much greater degree of accuracy than labouring through your deductive mind to find answers. If you find no answer springing to mind, it may be there is no answer to that question because it was not so relevant to this particular incident. On the other hand, it may mean that you are heavily defended in this area. If it feels like the question doesn't really matter, it is the former; but if you feel tense or upset, it is probably the latter. Just take some time to dwell meditatively on the subject until the answer unfolds.

This book works on spiritual if not religious principles, because the higher psychological principles are all spiritual. When I refer to 'Higher Mind' I am using a metaphor to describe an experience available to all of us from within. This term will be new to some people, and may take getting used to, especially by independent people who are used to doing it for themselves! But the 'Higher Mind' or 'Creative Mind' is a great time saver, and the most effective part of the mind. It also helps a person graduate into partnership and inter-dependence.

Some people, because of their religious background, are happier using certain words for God, Higher Power, Jesus, Buddha, Mohammed, Holy Spirit, etc. They are all referring to the same internal experience.

As you begin to use the Higher Mind, reactions to religious upbringing may surface as a natural part of the healing process. The term 'Higher Mind' can easily translate into your religious beliefs because the spiritual psychological principle employed transcends the metaphors of any particular religion. Whatever word you are comfortable with will work best for you, whether you call it 'Holy Spirit', 'Creative Mind' or 'Higher Power'.

So when I refer to Higher Mind I am referring to that part of the mind both spiritual and transcendent, whose job it is to take care of problems and conflicts for us. It is that part of us which knows all the answers. It is very powerful, and not employed as often as it could be. I have found it a major source of inspiration and information and used it to good effect when faced with major traps or conflicts. It makes any job easier, because it accomplishes through 'being' or grace, rather than doing.

While using this part of your mind may be unfamiliar at first, it is worth pursuing. I have found that the degree of difficulty in people's lives reflects the extent to which they are trying to do it themselves, rather than letting it be done through them.

It's best to work through this book completing one lesson a day, but if you do not have time to do a lesson every day, or if a lesson is so powerful you'd like to spend a couple of days on it, that's fine. It will not interfere with the process. Trust your instincts about how to use this book. You'll do fine. If you provide the willingness, miracles can happen.

After finding your perfect mate, you will notice these lessons and the principles within them are helpful in many other ways as well. Continue to apply them and they will help you keep your perfect mate.

After reading this book for the first time, you may want to re-explore the principles it contains. There are many ways to do this. One is just open the book and practise the principle on that page. A whole new life may open up for you. There's much to explore. I wish you the very best in your adventure. Happy relationship!

Before You Begin

This book is about many things. It is a primer in the psychology of the subconscious. It is a book about right relationships. But most of all it is a book to help you to allow yourself to find your perfect mate. And if for some reason you are not ready for your perfect mate, the principles will still work for finding your next relationship, or can even be extrapolated from to find your next job, or to assist you to take the next important step in your life.

Along with the principles explained in this book and offered to you as tools for your use, comes a certain amount of responsibility. You are asked to remember your integrity, for without it you cannot receive, feel, and therefore enjoy what you have manifested. For instance, to keep manifesting relationship after relationship, just so you can try them out, changes what is potentially our greatest source of growth, a relationship, into a game or a trap. Your game can be used to turn money, sex, power, relationships, success, etc., into much less than they are. Your ego likes to collect trophies to build itself up. Gaming is something we do instead of receiving and loving. Games substitute adrenalin and stimulation for happiness. A poor choice, but a common mistake in our society today.

As you begin these thirty days, please remember the importance of your growth now, and for the rest of your life. Creating your perfect mate is just the beginning. Then it is time to learn of love, intimacy, forgiveness, commitment, communication, letting go and all the other powerful lessons which enable a relationship to grow and unfold. Otherwise you will create perfect mate after perfect mate without being able to be intimate, to love and to enjoy your love.

It is important to recognise whether you are so independent or immature that you pillage the opposite sex. All that 'taking' does is gratify the ego and create an even greater inability to feel, enjoy and receive. It is a trap. You can grow out of this trap if you choose to move forward.

We have a great name for this kind of 'taking' in Hawaii. We call it 'cock-a-roaching': surreptitiously taking while pretending you don't need anything. We do this when we haven't yet recovered from our early wounds in our relationships or families.

You don't have to be perfect to have a relationship. If that were so, none of us would have one. But, as you go into a relationship, recognise your need for healing and be willing to let your partner help you. Surely the major purpose of your life is happiness – and this a relationship is able to provide. If you are not happy, then the next most important purpose, healing, is called for. A relationship reveals not only all that needs to be healed, but with a proper attitude and teamwork, it provides the support and means for the healing to take place.

Relationships offer the fastest means of growth – and

the biggest pitfalls. That's what makes relationships the central point of our lives with regard to happiness or distress, or any of the other key aspects of life such as health, money or success.

You don't have to believe in the principles for them to work. If you fully believed in them you wouldn't need this book. But it is important to read and practise these principles as best you can. There are a number of seminal principles and exercises, any of which could manifest your perfect mate. Combined together they create openness, willingness, attractiveness and creativity.

These principles and exercises have been developed over a dozen years of marriage counselling and over twenty-two years of work as a therapist. More importantly, I have tested them all personally. Now I offer them to you, as I have to friends and clients, so you can discover, as they have, that the key to freedom and happiness is within you.

Completing these thirty lessons is an investment in your greatness and fullness as a human being. The more you apply them, the more they will expand your consciousness, build your confidence and self-esteem. With this book you are setting out once more on a great adventure: to know yourself and to have the happy life you desire. Good Luck and Good Fortune to you!

Chuck Spezzano
May 1992
Hawaii

DAY 1

Your Mind is a Beautiful Thing

Your mind is a beautiful thing because it has limitless potential. Usually our lives are so bound by limits that at times we feel overwhelmed by all we seem to be up against. It is our nature to want to transcend our limits.

The Sufi mystic, Rumi, said we must take 70,000 steps of darkness into light to reach heaven. Whether that number is literally accurate or not, it contains a metaphoric truth about what it takes to reach an enlightened consciousness.

Our mind has the ability to heal, to realise truth, to manifest desires, to transcend time, to solve difficult life problems, and much, much more. Most people are afraid of the power of the mind, and remain trapped in situations as if attempting to prove they are powerless. But because I have worked with many thousands of victims, I know the mind's ability to find solutions in the most seemingly impossible situations. When people really are willing to find their way out of a situation, the answer, or at least the doorway to the answer, appears.

Scientists tell us we use 4 per cent of the mind's potential. In the 1970s people thought we probably used about 12 per cent, but in the last two decades we have reached a better understanding of the power of the mind. I call this 4 per cent the 'conscious mind'.

The part of your mind which supplies most of the answers is the Higher Mind. This is the best name for the part of our mind which has all the answers. Your whole life will get easier when you begin to work with that part of your mind, because its specific job is to solve your problems and it does so with such speed that it makes it seem as if our conscious mind is part of the problem, rather than, as you might think, part of the solution.

Today's Exercise

Every day, use the space provided to write down your answers or thoughts provoked by the exercises. You may also like to keep a daily diary of your progress towards your perfect mate.

1 Choose a problem in your life and write it down as specifically and concretely as you possibly can.

2 Experience any feelings associated with it.

3 Imagine you are willing and have the courage to find the solution.

4 Imagine turning this entire problem over to your Higher Mind. There are only two minds: your Higher Mind and your personality mind. The personality mind is totally devoted to making up a story about you and your specialness. You are making yourself special when you feel a lack of self-worth. The Higher Mind which knows your real value only wants to give you the grace to heal all your problems.

5 Be willing to do anything you are inspired to do to shift the problem. Whenever you think of the past, just know it is being handled for you. Getting the answer is easy. Not getting the answer is difficult.

DAY 1

My Daily Progress Towards My Perfect Mate

....

....

....

....

....

....

....

....

....

....

....

....

....

....

....

....

DAY 2

The Importance of Value

Value gives importance. Thus self-value gives you your experience of importance. Your life, your experience, and what the world deals out to you, all reflect your hidden feelings about your own value.

Unfortunately, the bad news is most people value themselves very little. The amount of guilt and unworthiness people experience leads them into sacrifice (which is the kind of giving that blocks receiving), to work hard rather than intelligently, and to live out roles (more of the same kind of giving which allows no receiving, and never lets the giver collect a reward). Roles lead to 'burn-out' and trying to compensate for a lack of self-value. That same lack of self-value drives people into doing, and doing, and doing. It does not allow peace, joy and abundance.

The good news is guilt and unworthiness are not the truth. Guilt is simply a mistake you beat yourself up for. Guilt keeps you stuck. It locks the mistake in place, preventing you from learning the lesson which can be naturally learned from it. Guilt causes the lack of self value you feel; at the deepest psychological levels guilt is a form of avoidance preventing you from growing. But all guilt can be resolved.

You deserve a lot more. It is your sense of self-value which ultimately allows you to attract a mate of similar value. Feelings of self-value also create the kind of experience you have with that mate. If you want a perfect mate, you must learn to let yourself be a perfect mate.

Today's Exercise

1 Today, become aware of what you think of yourself by how you act and by how the world acts towards you.

How I think of myself: ....

....

....

2 Notice when you are feeling unhappy and when you are compensating for feeling unhappy by sacrifice, by keeping busy, or by seeking mindless pleasure. These activities just hide places of valuelessness.

I feel unhappy when..

....

....

3 When you catch yourself in a situation which makes you aware of your lack of self-value, make a new decision about yourself.

The new decisions I have made: ....

....

....

Your power to choose is your greatest power. If you don't like what you're experiencing, begin by consciously choosing not to like the situation, and ask your Higher Mind quietly what is your real worth.

Listen.

The words from your Higher Mind always come with grace, which is to say that if your Higher Mind is telling you to be happy, you immediately feel happy. Your Higher Mind speaks with the purity of truth and you hear and experience it that way. Ask your Higher Mind to demonstrate to you your real worth. If you let your Higher Mind take over, within twenty-four hours even the most chronic situations can shift dramatically in a positive way.

Some people seek their self-value by having a partner. This is ultimately self-defeating, because what you look for outside yourself to prove your worth (by doing or having) covers up and maintains your lack of self-value. Your value is within you. It is demonstrated by how much you give of yourself and how much you let yourself receive.

I give my attention to, spend my time thinking about, and give up things so that I can...................................

....

These are all ways of attempting to hide feelings of valuelessness. Don't use your relationship to prove your value, but have a partner to create happiness for both of you. Choose your mate as a partner on your path of growth, a companion with whom to explore life's adventures and opportunities.

DAY 2

My Daily Progress Towards My Perfect Mate

DAY 3

The Purpose of Life

The purpose of life is happiness. Simple enough, but most of us take wrong turns on the Highway to Happiness. When we are not happy, then healing becomes our primary purpose. The purpose of a relationship is firstly happiness, and secondly, to heal. It does this through love, communication and forgiveness. When you are living your purpose you experience fulfilment. Each of us has a personal purpose which only we can fulfil.

Relationships provide the motivation and the fuel for completing our personal purpose – the means for us to reach happiness. They give us the support to heal ourselves as we progress through life. They expose our wounds from the past in order to make our continued growth possible. The past is relived in present relationship patterns, giving us the opportunity for healing. Heartbreak in a relationship has its roots in the past, and is a reliving of a past heartbreak, therefore as the past heartbreak is healed the present one heals too.

Today's Exercise

Your Higher Mind will help you live your purpose and realise your happiness. It has a plan for your happiness which will succeed. Be willing to let go of your plan for happiness. Look at how much of your plan has actually worked. Your subconscious intentions have clearly created other results than those your conscious mind intended. Here you have evidence of a split mind.

Your higher mind is a place of wholeness without ambivalence, and it unequivocally wants your happiness.

Let go of your plan for happiness and let your Higher Mind be in charge. Be willing to do anything you are inspired to do, but let your conscious mind be at rest. As you develop a relationship with your Higher Mind, you will become naturally more inter-dependent with those around you, including the person who will become your perfect mate. This is a natural prerequisite, not only to finding the perfect mate, but in keeping him or her. Remember your desire for the right relationship is a natural part of your purpose in life. You deserve your perfect mate and you deserve partnership.

What I really want is...

....

What I have is...

....

I am going to have what I truly deserve, the perfect partner and the best in life.

DAY 3

My Daily Progress Towards My Perfect Mate

....

....

....

....

....

....

....

....

....

....

....

....

....

....

....

....

DAY 4

You Have What You Want

With this lesson we begin our first major foray into the subconscious mind. What you have in your life is exactly what you want because that is what you have made and brought to you. The way to have something different is by changing your mind because that allows you to change your world.

One of the biggest traps we face in life is playing the role of victim, thinking we don't want what we have. Once you begin to realise you are making the choices, albeit at a subconscious level, you can start choices consciously, and have a much better chance of getting what you really want.

I have saved myself from death, a car accident, numerous colds and flu, simply because I became aware of that split-second decision which we always repress immediately to avoid taking responsibility. Through using this principle I've helped people from all walks of life free themselves from thousands of painful situations.

The first step is to look at the principle 'you have what you want', in the light of your own life. Consciously nobody wants pain, yet this morning a woman told me the only time she was at peace was after she hurt herself. Hurting herself was her way of attempting to pay off guilt. But self-inflicted punishment does not resolve or even lessen guilt. It is merely a stop-gap measure which doesn't work.

There are several key dynamics which create situations we appear not to want: fear, seeking attention (an attempt to get love or win back a relationship), getting our needs met (trying to be special or different), revenge, holding on to a past relationship, attacking someone while pretending to be innocent, trying to hold the family together, attempting to control someone or get them to sacrifice themselves for you, and many, many more.

One of the most common attitudes I find in single people who are avidly looking for a relationship (but failing to find one) is fear of losing their independence or freedom. They are unaware that paradoxically it is only through commitment that we experience true freedom.

As you begin to explore experiences in your life, especially why you don't have your perfect mate, many feelings may come up: anger, defensiveness, denial, guilt, hurt, doubt, shame, disbelief, and sadness. Just experience them and notice you are experiencing them. No negative feeling is ultimately accurate. This principle is the basis of all healing and is the reason why all painful feelings and situations can be transformed.

Remember, the purpose of examining the principle 'you have what you really want' is to free you from the invariable prisons, buried pain and the accompanying guilt which have been with you all along, just waiting for a chance to show themselves. As you experience negative emotions, try repeating the mantra, 'this feeling is not the truth.'

This type of exploration is the beginning of a journey of empowerment. Many people spontaneously recognise and free themselves of blocks just by applying this principle to their lives. Many answers just pop into their minds intuitively.

Today's Exercise

1 OK, you want your perfect mate. Yet something has
  been stopping you. This next exercise is a gem for
  helping the mind discover that blocking hidden
  agenda.

Step 1   Pretend for a moment you really don't want
a partner! Now, we know you do, but for the purpose of
this exercise pretend you don't. As soon as you can
imagine that, move on to the next step.

Step 2   Write down all the reasons which come into
your mind why you *don't* want a partner.

I don't want a partner because ....

....

Step 3   Consider what you have written as your subconscious agenda.

Step 4   Choose once again what it is you really want
in the light of this new information.

What I really want is:..

....

....

2 Answer the following questions to help you accept
  your accountability for what you have in your life at
  present. You will begin exploring your subconscious
  mind and the hidden 'benefits' you secretly derive

from situations you consciously don't want. These questions can be used to explore other areas of your life, but today concentrate on the question of the absence of a partner:

a) What does this allow me to do? Or, putting it another way, what does not having a mate allow me to do?

....

b) What is it I *don't* have to do as a result of not having a partner? ....

....

c) What is my purpose in not having a partner? ....

....

d) How does this make me special? ....

....

e) What am I afraid of? ....

....

f) What sacrifice am I afraid of? ....

....

g) What guilt am I paying off? ....

....

h) Why don't I feel I deserve a partner? ....

....

i) Who would I be untrue to, if I got my perfect mate?

....

j) Who am I getting revenge on by not succeeding in this? ....

....

Prioritise the questions which seem the most powerful to you.

The answer to any one of these questions can, depending on its content, stop you from having your perfect mate.

If you don't like the answers which have come up, as they are holding you back from having a partner, take a few moments to make some new choices.

I am turning over to my Higher Mind the following areas where I feel helpless and unable to change:

....

....

DAY 4

My Daily Progress Towards My Perfect Mate

....

....

....

....

....

....

....

....

....

....

....

....

....

....

....

....

....

....

DAY 5

Saying Yes to Life

To get what you want, your perfect mate, you will have to change. If you stay as you are, you will go on receiving what you have now. Change is one of the greatest blessings on earth, yet it is fear of change, or fear of the unknown, which most commonly blocks us. But to grow and reach our higher goals we must change.

I've worked with many people who would rather keep the devil they know than reach for the angel they don't. Years of studying the dynamics of relationship problems have taught me that fear, fear of the next step to be precise, is at the core of all problems.

Since most of your problems have the purpose of delaying your next step in order to protect you from your fear, when you take the next step it resolves the problem you are facing now.

Many people have said to me: 'Tell me what my next step is and I'll take it.' But, even when they know what it is, most people avoid taking their next step because of fear.

So we have to trust and take the next step forward, not knowing what it is, but reminding ourselves it will be better, just like every other step forward we have ever taken. Of course, taking the 'next step' isn't literally taking a step. It is being open to change, saying 'yes' to life. When this happens, life actually seems to change around us. One powerful way to look at life is to regard our major problems as fear of taking the next developmental step in life. That will help us to focus on the real issue rather than its numerous and confusing symptoms.

One of these major developmental steps, a crucial cornerstone step, is immediately before you now: the step of having your true partner. When you say 'yes' and are willing to take this step, you will open yourself up to new life and new horizons.

Today's Exercise

Sit quietly and close your eyes.

Imagine the next step awaits you and you can say 'yes' to it, 'yes' to change. You don't have to figure out what it is, or how to do it. All you have to do is want it, be willing for it to happen, knowing it will be better and further forward than where you are now. Take one step at a time. You can handle each step, especially with the help of your Higher Mind. Right now it's important to concentrate solely on what is before you.

Say YES to the next step. Say 'yes' to your perfect mate.

I am willing to take the next step towards finding my perfect mate.

It only takes an instant of sincerely choosing to have this happen.

DAY 5

My Daily Progress Towards My Perfect Mate

....
....
....
....
....
....
....
....
....
....
....
....
....
....
....
....
....
....

DAY 6

Opening the Door

Once, years ago, I broke up with a girlfriend. Our relationship had begun as a friendship and became something more. I had always thought we would retain that friendship no matter what happened. But when we did break up I felt that everything was lost. I can remember how angry I was at first, but I soon got over it.

I began looking around for eligible dating partners. It seemed as if all the eligible women had moved out of the city. I was a young doctor, athletic, romantic, attractive enough. Yet there were no eligible women around. I couldn't understand it.

Four and a half months went by, which was a record for me in not finding and dating someone I found attractive. At that time I became a support staff member at a three-and-a-half-day workshop. On the very last day of the workshop, while thinking of my lack of dating partners, I had an intuitive flash that I had slammed the relationship door at the end of the last one. I realised that was the reason I had met no one. So I decided to open the door and within the hour I had met someone I was attracted to, who let me know that she was very available. Within a week, I met two more very eligible dating partners and proceeded to make up for lost time.

This taught me a very important principle: relationships wait on invitation and not on time; your perfect mate awaits your invitation, not just a special time or place.

Today's Exercise

1 If you are not in a serious relationship, or haven't been in one for a while, take a look to see if you have slammed the door of relationships on your perfect mate – maybe after your last relationship, or even as a child with your parents.

2 Ask yourself: 'Am I ready for my perfect mate, or do I want more time to learn and build up confidence with light relationships along the way?'

It is important to accept wherever you are, as this will, paradoxically, help you to unfold and advance.

3 Consider whether you have ever opened the door to your perfect mate.

4 Imagine that you can feel or see the door inside you which you closed. See yourself walking to that door and doing whatever it takes to open it.

Remember this is your door: it will be any way you picture it. And as you open it you will experience a new openness which can last.

Just open your door.

Relax – enjoy yourself and feel the expectancy.

DAY 6

My Daily Progress Towards My Perfect Mate

....

....

....

....

....

....

....

....

....

....

....

....

....

....

....

....

....

....

DAY 7

The Power of Forgiveness

Many people prevent their perfect mate finding them because they are holding on to major grievances against their parents or old lovers. Such grievances lock you in the past. The anger or withdrawal that occurred then stops you from realising your present possibilities. Forgiveness frees us from the past.

Sometimes sacrifice is confused with forgiveness. People become afraid to forgive because they think if they do forgive, what they don't like will continue to happen to them. That is sacrifice, not forgiveness. Forgiveness releases you from the situation you don't want so that both the forgiver and the forgiven are freed. Forgiveness is the solvent that releases the super glue of grievances and guilt.

Judgement and grievance always hide subconscious guilt. Forgiveness releases the guilt, conscious or subconscious, which is part of every problem.

Grievances and guilt are distracting and can stop personal growth. Transform them through forgiveness and thus free yourself from unpleasant behaviour patterns which block your ability both to attract and to receive.

Today's Exercise

Today, allow to come to mind any problems or grievances, from the past or present, which may be holding you back from your perfect relationship. Under every problem or grievance is hidden guilt.

Allow the person, or persons, you need to forgive to come into your mind.

Be willing to free yourself and the person you are forgiving from the destructive power of that hidden guilt. Forgiveness releases us from that which we blame on others and ourselves. There are numerous forgiveness exercises. Here are two excellent ones:

1 Write down who, and what it is, you have a grievance about. Ask yourself: 'Would I blame myself for this?'

   If you can answer 'no' to this question, then both you and the person you were judging are released.

2 We can be very poor at forgiveness because, as human beings, we always want to be right. Being right always hides guilt and destroys happiness.

   The easiest form of forgiveness is to turn the grievance over to your Higher Mind to handle for you. Let your Higher Mind accomplish the forgiveness.

DAY 7

*My Daily Progress
Towards My Perfect Mate*

....
....
....
....
....
....
....
....
....
....
....
....
....
....
....
....
....
....

DAY 8

Feeling Your Feelings!

Your feelings add richness and dimension to your life and make you more attractive. You don't have to feel your feelings to manifest your perfect mate, but you do if you want to enjoy a long and happy relationship. Your ability to feel your feelings correlates with your ability to be a partner and to commit yourself to a relationship. But I want you to make a distinction between feeling your feelings and the amount of feeling you display.

Some people avoid their true feelings by expressing many kinds of other feelings. This can become a form of hysteria. Negative emotions are sometimes used as blackmail or revenge, or as a form of immaturity, depending on the way they are expressed. But just as an over-emphasis on your feelings or the expression of negative feeling can be counter-productive to good relationships and a form of avoidance, so can dissociation from your feelings.

A successful relationship is possible when we move from dependence and independence with others into inter-dependence. As we get in touch with our feelings we become more able to relate. Part of the movement from independence towards inter-dependence is being able to re-associate ourselves with our feelings and our body. And as we get in touch with our negative feelings and release them, our ability to receive and experience increases.

It takes courage for someone to move towards inter-dependence because of the amount of suppressed and repressed emotion we discover that we have to move through on the way. Feeling our feelings lessens self-denial, makes our subconscious mind more conscious, and increases both our honesty and integrity. All of which makes us more attractive.

Today's Exercise

One of the simplest forms of healing is to experience your negative feelings or emotions until they disappear. You can do this whenever you are not feeling great.

All you do is allow yourself to feel the feelings as intensely as possible, even exaggerate them.

Observe everything about your feelings, explore the minute and distinct sensation of each emotion. You will find that as you do they will begin to shift.

Once started, don't stop until you are feeling great.

Feelings, even the most chronic ones, have an end.

Even if you hit a gusher of repressed emotion, it is unlikely to last more than a few days. But you will be happier, feel healthier and be more able to receive afterwards. Experiencing your negative emotions until they are gone heals and moves you forward in your life.

If in this exercise you hit a feeling of deadness or emptiness, or nothingness, or you just feel blocked, and have hard-to-identify non-feelings, that's fine. Strangely enough, they are all kinds of feelings too. Just feel them until they transform and you can move to the next level. Most of us are afraid of negative emotions. But this simple tool, truly feeling your feelings, will give you an attractive courage and maturity.

Practise feeling your feelings all day today. You can do that and do everything else.

Today, experiment, and follow at least one negative feeling all the way through to a good feeling.

What I have learned about my feelings........................

....

The positive feelings I expressed today were when......

....

DAY 8

My Daily Progress Towards My Perfect Mate

....
....
....
....
....
....
....
....
....
....
....
....
....
....
....
....
....
....

DAY 9

The Truth Will Set You Free!

Many people are frightened of relationships because they are afraid of sacrifice. They fear they will become a love-slave in the way they did in the past, and that is enough to keep anybody independent.

Yet the extent of your independence is a reflection of the amount of sacrifice and dependency you still need to heal. In a successful relationship all three of these roles, sacrifice, dependency and independence are healed. If you want to grow as a person, you will have to face these cornerstone roles sooner or later.

These roles begin in childhood with a trauma, some kind of emotional loss, which was never resolved or mourned. The role becomes a pattern which typically repeats itself in your life. All three roles – sacrifice, dependency and independence – are surreptitious forms of taking combined with an inability to receive. If we fail to resolve these counter-productive roles, deadness in our relationships is the inevitable result.

Not knowing how to handle deadness and boredom keeps many people out of committed relationships, or relationships altogether. Yet for a successful relationship and life, they have to be handled. You have to learn these lessons sometime. Through many years of studying deadness in relationships, I have discovered a number of ways of healing, transcending or resolving the deadness.

The bottom line is deadness can be healed because it never is the real truth. It is just something to heal.

Deadness is a cocoon we have woven and wrapped around ourselves to keep out emotional pain. It is a form of control to prevent things or people coming to mean so much to us that we can be hurt – again. Deadness lets others know we are 'special' and subtly, or not so subtly, is a form of attack.

Deadness comes out of our roles, rules and duties – doing the right thing for the wrong reasons. It is a place of blindness and deafness to the world and relationships around us. In the deadness we have gained so much control, become so sure we have the answers, that we limit the input from the outside world to almost nothing. Roles are a failure to make contact while looking like you are in contact; living life from rules, but as good as those rules may seem, they begin to get old. Life cannot be lived from rules; they destroy your ability for intimacy and authenticity.

Secondly, fusion creates deadness. Fusion is not knowing the boundaries between you and others. When they feel pain you suffer. Fusion, or over-closeness, automatically suggests sacrifice which falsifies giving and disallows receiving.

We have a great deal of fusion that needs healing in our relationships. As children, there was often one parent with whom we didn't get on so well while with the other we were extremely close and in 'fusion'. This is the parent with whom we have deeply hidden issues because our feelings are so powerful that we cannot communicate. Fusion leads through sacrifice to 'burn-out', to feelings of repulsion, or even revulsion.

Two well-hidden causes of deadness are competition and 'fear of the next step'. If you believe you are the best, it creates a subtle (or not so subtle) atmosphere in your relationships that communicates to others that there is no equality and therefore no risk of intimacy. Some people win the competition game so strongly they have no space for a partner even though they are seeking one. Once you are the best, there is no room for anyone else.

How much someone means to you generates both your feelings and their value to you, making you feel alive and at the same time aware of the risk of loss. It is the possibility of our partners becoming too important, meaning too much that breeds aliveness in a relationship but when we are afraid of feeling that intensely we seek to control and become afraid to take the next step with our partners.

Fear of the next step leads to a sameness that is deadening. One of the easiest ways to move through feelings of deadness is just to be more willing to move forward in your life. It is that willingness which creates change, because life changes as you become ready for it to change.

Dissociation from your feelings is the last aspect I shall mention here which creates the experience of deadness. Severe deadness in a relationship, or in yourself, speaks of extreme feelings which have been repressed.

Some feelings are so painful that we forget them, then forget that we have forgotten them.

These feelings are so painful that we would feel like dying were we to discover them. But they are waiting to be healed and your willingness alone can take you into the old storehouse of feelings.

There is a simple way to heal feelings that hurt that bad – service. Whenever you feel so bad that you want to die, if you give or choose to be in service to another, those feelings become a birth, instead of a death, situation. Much more could be said about how to heal deadness, but if the principles above are followed, you will find a way through.

Today's Exercise

Today, use truth as an indicator of your happiness. Truth is a major antidote to feelings of deadness. When something feels dead, truth is being avoided. Happiness is our deepest, truest consciousness; if you are feeling unhappy, it is not the truth. As our problems are resolved, we are led to happiness and as our consciousness grows, so does our happiness. If you are not happy, ask for the truth to be shown to you.

Seek the truth. Desire the truth. It will set you free.

Today, ask for the truth to be shown to you in such a manner you will recognise it and be released. Make truth your ally. Ask to be shown the truth. Listen both within, and to others, and see what the world brings you.

The truth about my relationship with ....
is..

The truth about my present and past relationships with partners is..
....
....

My progress towards my perfect mate ....
....

DAY 9

My Daily Progress Towards My Perfect Mate

....

....

....

....

....

....

....

....

....

....

....

....

....

....

....

....

....

....

DAY 10

Letting Go of the Past Opens Up the Present

Once again we have reached a seminal lesson in the process of finding your perfect mate – the principle of letting go. Letting go counters the destructive influence of holding on.

Holding on, or attachment, is needed in the disguise of love. It is a form of counterfeit love which leads to a blurring of personal boundaries between you and the one to whom you are attached. This leads to fusion and sacrifice, which creates feelings of deadness in relationships. The extent of your attachment in relationships is the extent of your unattractiveness, and repels your partner. What keeps you attractive in a relationship is your letting go of attachment and needs.

But you must distinguish letting go from throwing away, or dissociation. Letting go is a willingness to give up our attachments, so you can feel connection and love with your partner. When your partner becomes independent and needs more space, you are becoming dependent and are called upon to let go. Whenever you let go, your relationship can move forward to the next step in partnership, confidence, and love.

Letting go is not throwing away; it is putting in perspective. Letting go is like having the best secretary in the world filing away past papers, so your desk is clear. If anything is needed again you can easily retrieve it.

It is critical to consider letting go to find your perfect mate. If you do not let go of previous relationships, you have barriers up blocking beginning one again.

What you hold on to from the past, you do not allow in your present.

Every anger, hatred, grievance, sadness, and heartbreak you fantasise over, and hold on to, prevents you from enjoying yourself.

Relationships from the past which may be blocking you include your parent and siblings of the opposite sex. Your attachment to them, which gets in the way of your love for them, blocks you from having a relationship, or limits the quality of that relationship. Joy comes from living in the present – there is no joy living in the past.

At a more conscious level, negative feelings are just an incomplete grieving process. Nobody is fully ready to begin anew until they have let go, and finished with, the feelings involved in grieving over the past. At the deepest level of our subconscious, we have these feelings as an attempt to protect ourselves. They are a self-conspiracy we use when we fear the next step.

Before the loss occurred, there was always some fear we didn't want to face; and, because we didn't face it then, the pain is still within us now. Face it and let it go, because letting go of the pain resolves the fear.

This type of personal conspiracy, subconsciously using pain or problems to keep us from moving forward, is at the heart of all our problems. It is a counter-productive way of dealing with fear because the fear remains. In letting go, the past is resolved. In trust, the present is approached with confidence.

We can never succeed in a relationship without letting go. Letting go is a paradoxical power of the utmost importance in a relationship. When we have need and attachment, we make demands on those around us to handle those needs for us which drives away those we love and feel we need so much.

Holding on keeps us unattractive. Letting go enhances our attractiveness. Letting go allows everything you prized in past relationships to be available to you in your future relationships.

Today's Exercise

Use your intuition as you answer the questions in this exercise. If an answer does not readily occur to you, guess.

Step 1   Imagine a bucket called 'The Bucket of Relationships'. Estimate the percentage you are holding onto someone, positively or negatively, and drop it into the bucket. For instance, if you are holding on to the parent of the opposite sex at the level of 50 per cent, put that in your bucket.

Add 'holdings' with your opposite-sex siblings, ex-lovers, favourite fantasy figures and opposite-sex children if you have any.

Your bucket may begin to look like this:

> 25 per cent – first love
> 10 per cent – opposite-sex siblings
> 20 per cent – opposite-sex parent
> 5 per cent – favourite star

Total: 60 per cent filled.

Even though your bucket starts overflowing, keep on going till you have listed the last one. It's often the case that it overflows. Consider your Relationship Bucket with reference to your present life experience and the extent of your independence.

How full is your bucket? Its emptiness is the extent to which you are open to a relationship, or are only open to one of poor quality. The person in the example above only has the potential for a 40 per cent relationship.

I once worked with someone in a workshop whose bucket was filled to 1,035 per cent. That meant, at best, she was only able to draw a man who represented a –935 per cent relationship. It became very clear to her why she was drawing in such lousy choices for partners. She made some new choices about letting go and her life changed for the better.

Step 2   Today is a great day for letting go of old relationships; here are some ways to do it:

Experience any negative feelings until only a positive feeling is left from the past.

Forgive.

Take a next step.

Recognise living in the past is destructive, and choose to live in the present.

Give up attachment, so you can have love.

Turn these relationships over to your Higher Mind to let go for you.

DAY 10

My Daily Progress
Towards My Perfect Mate

DAY 11

You Can Have What You Want – If You Want What You Have!

Today we will look at two very important concepts: acceptance and letting go.

The title has a double significance about acceptance. If you accept what you have, therefore, you naturally have what you want, but also if you do not resist what you have then what you want can come to you. What you resist persists. When you resist what you have, everything jams and cannot move forward.

Conversely, what you accept changes. Acceptance is not a form of apathy, but an active principle for healing resistance and pain.

In some of the most successful chronic pain institutes of North America, people who have had major accidents, suffer from arthritis or other forms of disease are taught to accept and experience their pain, rather than fight it. This simple method is highly effective in lessening pain.

Acceptance gets our lives moving again when they have become stuck; the power of acceptance moves life forward. Sometimes because of hurt, heartbreak, or feelings of rejection, we keep ourselves defended or quit relationships altogether.

Hurt does not come from what others do or don't do to us but from how we react to what they do. When we finally realise the truth – whether or not someone else is rejecting us – it is *our* rejection of ourselves which creates the hurt, then we are in charge of our feelings.

The Buddha's advice for Enlightenment is simple: 'Desire nothing; resist nothing.' Acceptance of reality allows life with regard to relationships to unfold once again.

Letting go is the other key aspect of this important lesson. If you have an expectation, you will stop yourself from moving forward. If you hear yourself saying 'should, 'have to', 'got to', 'need to', 'ought to' or 'must', you have expectations. If you 'need to' or 'have to' have a partner, typically you just can't find one. But paradoxically, when you don't need one, there are plenty around.

Your expectations are demands on others and who wants to feel demands? If you expect things from life you will be frustrated or disappointed. If you don't 'need' something, life often gives you as much of it as you want. Your willingness to give up 'needing' a partner, allows you to have one. Instead, *choose* to have or want a partner. The energy shift your new attitude will bring adds to your attractiveness.

Today's Exercise

1 Review your life for major hurts.

My list of major hurts: ....

....

....

Choose to accept, rather than deny or hide them, so that where your life has stopped it can begin to unfold again.

Affirm that being stopped by these old hurts is not what you want.

2 Accepting the experience of major difficulties can actually catapult us into higher consciousness and thus much greater happiness.

Today, turn over to your Higher Mind any experience you find impossible to accept.

If you feel hurt, you are in rejection. What is it you have difficulty accepting?

I have difficulty accepting ....

....

....

Realise hurt is only a mistake which can be corrected and does not have to stop you in this area of your life.

What I want now is ....

....

3 Life is teaching you you don't *need* anything outside yourself. Neediness and expectations are two of the major culprits in chasing partners away. This is not a form of independence, but a way of recognising that your happiness comes from within you.

Let go of any feelings of having to have a partner.

Trade expectations for a feeling of expectancy. Know your perfect partner is coming your way. Don't make demands and frighten him or her away.
Invite your partner in – know your partner is coming.

You'll be pleased with the results!

DAY 11

My Daily Progress Towards My Perfect Mate

....

....

....

....

....

....

....

....

....

....

....

....

....

....

....

....

....

DAY 12

Guilt, Unworthiness and Fear Are Merely Illusions

All negative emotions are illusions. Certainly we experience them and they affect us and sometimes even kill us. But, the good news is, these feelings are an illusion.

Painful feelings are an indication that something is amiss. I've worked with tens of thousands of people around the world and I have yet to find anyone, with any kind of willingness, who was unable resolve the blackest guilt, the deepest pain or the greatest fear.

The basis of the mind is happiness, or wholeness, and it is that wholeness which allows and promotes our continued movement towards growth and healing. When you penetrate the blocks to your subconscious, unconscious, or even Higher Mind, you will find yourself in the joy, breakthrough, or ecstasy of transcending. All negative feelings can be measured against those profoundly happy feelings to evaluate if they are true.

I've encountered many people who thought they were to blame for problem situations in their families while they were growing up, or for other dilemmas they encountered in life. They thought they were so guilty that they did not deserve to have a partner.

I've met many others who thought so poorly about themselves they believed they were unworthy of a partner. Others, who wanted a partner, were afraid to have one, because they felt they were too inadequate to be intimate. They were afraid that when their partners got to know them, they would leave them.

These feelings can be corrected fairly easily. Know that even though you are experiencing such feelings they are not accurate. These feelings, which can block you from finding a partner and destroy relationships, are not the truth. They can be resolved if you are willing to find the way past them, and change, so your life can be better.

Today's Exercise

1 Make a personal inventory of all the negative feelings which may stop you from finding your perfect mate.

2 Ask your Higher Mind to show you the way through these feelings or problems.

3 Don't make a monument to a mistake. Don't let mistakes be the super glue which stops you moving forward. If you are willing to change, a better life awaits you. Choose the truth.

4 If you give up your 'need' to have the answers, or to have events turn out in a certain way, and stop holding on to grievances or negative perceptions, you will experience peace and be free. As you change your perceptions you will find the whole situation and the people around you will also change.

5 If you don't feel motivated to make another choice, look for where you are still attached to the pain.

Answer: 'What is my purpose for holding on to this emotion or problem? My purpose is ....

Do I really want this to hold back my life and happiness? ....

I am choosing to have...
....

DAY 12

My Daily Progress
Towards My Perfect Mate

....

....

....

....

....

....

....

....

....

....

....

....

....

....

....

....

DAY 13

Freeing Yourself from Your Life of Fantasy

Here's another important lesson about how you may be blocking yourself from finding your perfect mate.

Everyone this side of enlightenment fantasises. There is nothing wrong with fantasising. In fact most human experience takes place in the imagination. When we think we need something, we fantasise. We begin to daydream about it. When we are hungry, we begin to think about food and notice all the cues related to food around us. Fantasy is an attempt to make up for what is missing within, or outside, you and gives a certain small satisfaction. But it does not really work because it is a defence and all defences cause the very thing you are attempting to defend yourself against.

To your mind, everything is a picture. Your mind cannot distinguish between you actually doing something and just thinking about it. So, if you are having sex, or merely imagining you are having sex, your mind does not know the difference.

If you fantasise about your perfect mate, you will often give yourself enough satisfaction; you won't bother to open yourself up for a real relationship. You can create a level of dissatisfaction within a relationship with the continued use of fantasy. Fantasy is using your imagination to make up for something missing. The more you fantasise, the more illusions you place between yourself and your partner. As your partner cannot live up to your fantasies, a growing sense of dissatisfaction, disappointment and frustration becomes inevitable. Be careful: if you let fantasy grow in your relationship, your attempts to make your partner more exciting will actually push your partner away.

Fantasy is based on loss, pain, grievance, and the judgement that something is missing in your life. Fantasy is an attempt to provide something that can only be achieved by joining with your partner at a new level of intimacy. Fantasy hides the crucial need to take the next step. When you fantasise, you are stuck and attempting to be satisfied by an illusion. Ultimately it won't work. Let go of your fantasies so you can experience the real thing in a way that satisfies you.

Today's Exercise

Step 1 When you catch yourself in a fantasy today, find out what is underneath it. Somewhere it is hiding a painful feeling which is acting as a wedge between you and your partner.

Step 2 Let go of any painful feeling by experiencing it until it is complete, or by handing it over to your Higher Mind.

Step 3 Recognise the pain for which your fantasies are compensating before turning them, especially those involving your perfect mate, over to your Higher Self.

My fantasy ....

....

The pain it was hiding was ....

....

I am ready for the next step!

DAY 13

My Daily Progress
Towards My Perfect Mate

If It Hurts,
It Isn't Love

Contrary to many popular and traditional songs, love does not hurt, but 'needs' do. Your past heartbreaks were really frustrations of your needs – part of a power struggle, where you used your hurt as a form of emotional blackmail to force your partner to do what you wanted and meet your needs. Your heartbreaks are really acts of revenge through which your pain declares the true, terrible character of your partner.

When you understand the dynamics of hurt and rejection you can take a giant stride towards maturity and you will open up to relationships, and to being a better partner, once you find your mate. Hurt is an attempt to make someone wrong. It results from something you cannot accept, that you resist, or reject. What you push away from you creates the hurt and emotional pain. Then, guess what, you project the pushing away on to your partner and feel rejected.

Projection is a defence. Projection is taking something you are doing and accusing someone else of doing it. Hurt results from giving to take, a form of sacrifice used to coerce your partner. When your partner pushes you away for taking, you get upset, which hides what you are doing.

Using hurt or heartbreak, as part of your conspiracy to gain control and thus do what you want in life, can be harmful to you both in finding a relationship and keeping one healthy.

Today's Exercise

If you have any experience which still hurts, discover the control that hurt is giving you. Would you rather have that control, or the perfect mate?

My experiences which still hurt ....

....

Through this hurt I am controlling..............................

....

Control is the part of independence that leads to fights. It is universally unattractive except to those looking for someone to take care of their needs. The openness of intimacy is rich and attractive to others.

Openness may be a risk but it is also the excitement and ability to enjoy. Your change is your cure.

What I really want ....

....

I will be happy when I have ....

....

DAY 14

My Daily Progress
Towards My Perfect Mate

....

....

....

....

....

....

....

....

....

....

....

....

....

....

....

DAY 15

Trust

Trust is one of the cornerstones of a relationship. There is no love without trust. Trust is the opposite of naivety, which is denial parading as innocence. When you trust you turn the power of your mind towards that which you are trusting, in an attitude of confidence, power and success. Trust is one of the core healing principles. Trust can resolve any problem.

A problem comes about because, given the nature of your subconscious, your mind is split. Whenever you are hurt in a major way, you fragment a piece of your mind and reject that part as painful. The fragmented part is projected outward and comes back to meet you as the problem. When this happens you adopt an attitude of control to keep the pain away from you. When you put trust into a negative situation, it begins to work for you and the situation unfolds in a positive way.

Control is a subtle form of power struggle which blocks relationships and indicates a fear of intimacy. It is the opposite of trust. Control attempts to take into its own power that which trust brings about by opening things up and clearing the way for resolution.

Today's Exercise

1 Today, every time you think of your perfect mate, know your perfect mate is coming to you. Trust yourself and your partner. As you put trust into the relationship, it will unfold as you do.

2 Possibly there is a part of you which wants a relationship and another which is afraid to have one.

Imagine holding these two parts, one in each hand.

Feel their weight and texture.

See or sense their colour, size, and shapes.

Smell their aromas.

Hear any sounds they make.

Imagine they are melting down to their pure energy – the basic building block of the universe.

Notice that when they are completely melted down the two handfuls are exactly the same.

Join the two handfuls of energy, so that when they are completely joined your fingers are interlocked.

Notice the new feeling, or form, emerging from the integration gives you your mind back – whole.

DAY 15

My Daily Progress
Towards My Perfect Mate

....

....

....

....

....

....

....

....

....

....

....

....

....

....

....

....

DAY 16

Manifesting Your Life

This is one of the three most important seminal lessons in finding your perfect mate. Do it well!

To manifest something you simply create what you want to happen. We do it all the time subconsciously. People who are good at manifesting what they want are those who know they have the power and use it consciously.

Everything, including the negative stuff, happens because we choose it. Today's lesson could change the rest of your life if you make this principle a part of your life.

When I was young and single and thought that fun was dating different women, I used to make lists of the attributes I wanted in my woman. The lists were long and specific describing characteristics, time available, etc., so that it would take months for my exact order to come to me. But she always did come with those specific details. If I had been more mature I might have been able to feel and enjoy those relationships more.

Manifesting is choosing to have something occur and it does. You could be choosing what you want to have happen at any time of day. The times the mind is most receptive is in the twilight sleep zones: just before you fall asleep and just before you get up.

That's the time to tell yourself the kinds of feelings and experiences you want to have during the coming day or in the near future. If you find something occurs which you do not like, then choose your preference again.

If something negative happens, then:

1 Acknowledge that you did not want it.

2 Acknowledge that you made a subconscious if not a conscious mistake in your choice.

3 Realise you deserve better outcomes.

4 Know if it's unhappy it is not the truth.

5 Choose once again what you want.

6 And turn it over to your Higher Self.

This one principle could keep you in happiness for the rest of your life.

Choose situations in which everyone wins, and keep your integrity.

Never choose someone else's partner, because that would create problems, guilt and delay for all concerned. And you might miss out on someone meant specifically for you. Your true partner will come to you unencumbered.

Remember to manifest happy things like health and abundance for those around you. What you manifest for others is manifested for you. How you bless others is how you are blessed.

Today's Exercise

List the qualities you want in your partner: ....

....

....

....

I intend to recognise my perfect mate.

Leave it open enough for anything else that your Higher Mind might want to include for your happiness.

Experience the energy of your request, how good it feels, and send it out into the universe, knowing your partner will soon be there.

Any time you think of your partner, know your partner is coming to you. Have gratitude both for what you have and what is coming. Don't worry about not doing it exactly right. It is not the way that you do it which counts, but your intention. I've heard of at least half a dozen ways of doing this and they all worked. This is the essence. When you have finished let your Higher Mind handle it for you. You may develop a style which works better for you. Trust yourself. And good luck.

DAY 16

My Daily Progress Towards My Perfect Mate

....
....
....
....
....
....
....
....
....
....
....
....
....
....
....
....
....
....
....
....

DAY 17

Your Attitude Is Your Direction

Your attitude is the most fundamental aspect of your life because it defines your direction. Your attitude is made up of your decisions, all moving in the same general direction. It's important to know what you want, where you want to go, to set goals, and make good decisions to support that goal (and you may have to be courageous and take a few risks).

You will need to change for you to have your perfect mate, or even for you to be happy with your perfect mate. Change is inevitable if you want to succeed, because – just think for a moment – if you go on doing what you've been doing, you'll go on getting more of what you've already got. Your attitude towards change is crucial to your success. If you are in pain, or feeling the deadness, you may begin to recognise change as the greatest blessing on earth. Why don't you just decide that any change will be exciting or a great adventure?

It is important to choose not only to have your perfect mate, but to be happy with him or her. This may seem obvious, but without choosing that second goal your first major misunderstanding may be your last. Once you have chosen your goal for the relationship anything which comes up is just something to work out on your way to happiness.

There are problems and situations to work on and heal in every relationship. Everything between you and total joy will come up between you and your partner, because old pain and behaviour patterns disguise themselves as problems in present relationships and lead us into fights or deadness. So have a healing attitude in your relationship.

If anything is not love, it is a call for help.

This thought helps us look beyond negative behaviour to what is underneath and respond with love and understanding. When you find your perfect mate, believe me, the journey is just beginning.

Romance is the first stage in a relationship. It is swiftly followed by two, not such fun, phases: the Power Struggle and the Dead Zone before you move into Co-creation.

Many relationships don't make it through the Dead Zone. Major falling outs and breakups happen during the Power Struggle. Your attitude towards and understanding of these stages is crucially important to help your relationship thrive.

Choose to become an expert in intimacy, love, communication, trust, letting go and forgiveness. Then, not only will your relationship move forward, your whole life may move forward in leaps and bounds. Decide your relationship will be about more than just you and your feelings, but about truth and healing. That choice alone could save you from years of dead ends and delays in which you are subtly, or not so subtly, taking control or making *you* the most important part of your relationship. Given the complexity of the human mind, there are literally thousands of things of a very complicated nature and simple things of profound dimensions to heal in a relationship. They can all be healed (and simply), if there is true desire and a willingness to move forward.

Step by step, your ease and confidence will grow as you mature. Choose to learn your relationship lessons quickly and easily.

Make sure your partner always wins 100 per cent alongside you. If you don't, you will end up paying the bill, by sacrifice or by the loss of your partner's attractiveness. Choose to learn joyfully and remove the ways which separate you and your partner.

Today's Exercise

Take a long look at your life.

Where are you heading?

It's time to change, to work to eliminate choices, prejudices, or fear which may be holding you back.

Choose goals and attitudes for your relationship that will support your use of this most powerful vehicle of healing for your mutual growth and happiness.

My new goals and attitudes are ....

....

I deserve the best!

DAY 17

My Daily Progress
Towards My Perfect Mate

....

....

....

....

....

....

....

....

....

....

....

....

....

....

....

DAY 18

Free Your Family, Free Yourself

After years of researching what sets up life patterns, and the seemingly never-ending self-generating wellsprings of guilt that flood out of the subconscious mind, a number of things have become evident to me. Guilt blocks abundance and receiving, simultaneously generating self-attack and attacks and problems which seem to come from the outside world. No matter how much is cleared, there always seems to be more and more guilt.

Guilt is a major dynamic in all problems, including scarcity, but the more innocent we recognise ourselves to be, the easier and more abundant our life gets. Over the years I've learned there are areas in the subconscious where guilt seems to come up layer after layer, stopping people from growth and generating negative life patterns. I discovered these patterns begin in the family and often begin with experiences in the womb. I became aware of a number of dynamics common to these events.

The first is that these events become part of our personal conspiracies to stop our own greatness. We get frightened of the next step in our unfolding, and when we are about to take that step we subconsciously manifest a drama which blocks us. Typically, this is (or was) a trauma which involves members of our family.

Over two decades of therapy, I discovered that we seem to have to come *to heal the very problems or situations that traumatised us.*

We are the grace bringers – the gift-givers – by which I mean we have the ability through our 'beingness' to heal the problems which trap us in our families. When we are in a state of 'beingness' things work out, but when we blame others or ourselves or get trapped into feelings of sacrifice, we fail. And then we work harder, do more, compensate to try to prove we are good and successful people.

Unfortunately, we become caught up by the very problems and uneasiness that we came to heal. Typically, in the face of some overwhelming family problem, we begin to blame ourselves rather than recognise the gift we came to deliver.

Specifically, we came to save each of our family members, our parents as a couple, and our family as a whole. Each child comes in to help and support the child who has come before in a sort of rescue mission. Yet this is typically misunderstood by us. Research shows the birth of a sibling can be one of the most painful experiences a person goes through in life, rather than the welcoming of a friend and ally.

As children, we began to blame ourselves. We left our centre to try to resolve our problems. When we left our centres, we entered illusion and sacrifice, taking on a 'job' in an attempt to help. This 'job' is something we feel we have to do for someone in the family, like making them happy, or making lots of money for them or stopping them being angry. We may be enslaved or rebel against doing it, but we are caught by it.

Unfortunately we could never succeed at the job, and that generated guilt. Out of fear we 'do' the job ourselves rather than allowing it to be done through grace or just through our beingness. Repeatedly we left our centres, that place of innocence and simplicity, unaware that it could lead to self-destruction and even death of that self.

The mind, being resilient, willingly begins a new self for us, but begins it from off our centre, in a guilty, unreceiving place.

Blaming ourselves, feeling guilty, we go off our centres trying to make the problem better by our sacrifice. This leads to taking on a 'job', doingness, compensation for the guilt by hard work. This causes difficulty, fusion and competition in our lives.

When I finally understood this dynamic, the solution looked simple. It works this way. With the help of the Higher Mind (as the process could take weeks or even months without it), we can be carried back into our centres. Each of our family members can at our request be carried back to their centres.

Returning to our centres resolves long-standing guilt and removes negative life patterns. Since the purpose of guilt is to stop us moving forward, those guilt-related blocks produce life patterns which stop our personal purpose. Once these blocks are resolved in our families, then we can naturally give our gift to the world. If your self has 'died', imagine breathing life back into it so it can come alive again. Then it can be carried back into your centre and be reintegrated.

Your gift is not necessarily something you do. It is something you embody naturally. It proceeds in grace from your being, and creates more ease and success in your life.

Today's Exercise

List the major grievances you have towards people in your family, both living and dead: ....

....

....

This is what you came to help them with and even save them from. Each grievance stops you unfolding and your natural movement forward. These grievances hide your guilt and lock you into sacrifice in some form of unsuccessful pattern. So be willing to forgive the person with whom you had a grievance by not using that person to hold yourself back.

Imagine taking the hand of each person you had a grievance with, and see yourself walking forward, arm in arm, into the next stage of your life. You are no longer stuck with them, each step will realise a gift which has been waiting for you since the grievance began.

This process will work even if the person has died because it has a freeing effect on the life and karmic patterns of everyone involved and re-establishes personal value.

I am becoming free!

DAY 18

My Daily Progress
Towards My Perfect Mate

DAY 19

Roles, Rules and Duties

Roles and duties are about doing the right things for the wrong reasons. We drop into roles for approval, perform our expected duties to prove we are good, and to show others, usually our parents, how they should have acted in order to treat us right.

Roles and duties are based on grievances, feelings of guilt and failure. They are embodied forms of sacrifice and compensate us for our painful feelings.

Roles are like suits of armour, encasing us, cutting us off from intimacy, our ability to give and receive. Roles create deadness. The two most common roles are 'being good' and 'being a hard worker'.

In our society, the age at which most trauma happens appears to be about three years old, when we take on most of our roles. Roles and duties are forms of character, which while helping a child survive, can kill an adult. The higher ways of being for a child are love, creativity, giving and receiving, but these are not present in roles; neither are commitment, truth, ease, and freedom. Interestingly enough, fear of commitment is actually a fear of sacrifice, which results from living out roles, 'doing what is expected even if I don't like it'.

Paradoxically, true commitment creates freedom, release and ease because it emerges from choice.

Giving and receiving increases our sense of self-worth and heals the main dynamic of fear of commitment, which is that no one, including ourselves, is worthy of continuous attention.

Rules are built on guilt and pain. They have the same dynamics as roles and duties. They are rigid demands on ourselves and others, which lead to no-win situations, because if someone follows your rules, you feel a bit safer but still have the fear that generated those rules. Rules are counterfeit principles.

Principles flow and are life generating, beginning dialogue not ending it. Each of us has hundreds of contradictory rules about relationships. They are our attempts to keep ourselves safe, but, in the end, they separate us from our loved ones.

Today's Exercise

1 Look for all the areas in which you are giving, but don't seem to be receiving. Giving and receiving is a natural cycle, giving leads to receiving. An area where you are not receiving is an area in which you are in a role. To change a role into true giving just *choose* to give rather than giving because you are supposed to.

The areas in which I am giving and not receiving:.......

....

....

....

2 Make a list of all your rules which apply to the areas where you would feel hurt, upset or insulted if your rules weren't kept, e.g. infidelity, tardiness, insensitivity. To find these rules, think back to the times you felt hurt. As you find your rules, make new choices about the ones you feel ready to let go of. Turn those rules over to your Higher Mind to change into principles. A rule is rigid but a principle is flexible, which may be why people say that 'rules are meant to be broken'.

A rule hides old pain and guilt and is really a defence begging to be attacked so that the pain and guilt can be healed. Typically, when a rule is broken and we experience pain in a relationship, we adopt a reactive, defensive or attacking posture to protect ourselves rather than using the opportunity for communication, healing and evolution.

My rules are:..

....

....

....

3 Look closely at your roles or rules which may be preventing you from having a relationship.

The roles I am willing to change: ....

....

The rules I am willing to change: ....

....

....

I am making good choices!

DAY 19

My Daily Progress
Towards My Perfect Mate

Family Roles

Family roles can stop you having your perfect mate. They can block many of the good things in life. The major family roles are the hero, the martyr, the scapegoat, the lost child and the charmer. The hero, martyr and scapegoat are all guilt induced, while the charmer and the lost child are generated by feelings of inadequacy.

The hero is the shining light in the family, always succeeding, always winning, being good at sports, getting excellent grades, etc. The hero is the person in the family of whom everyone is proud. Heroes are trying to save the family by being the very best. Unfortunately, it is only a compensation for feeling guilty.

The scapegoat is the problem person in the family and always in lots of trouble. Scapegoats attempt to help the family by bringing all the trouble of the family on their own shoulders and trying to save it through their calls for help to outside agencies such as the police. They try to distract the family from its problems. This is their contribution to the family and it is a compensation for guilt.

The martyr becomes sick or has problems in an

attempt to swallow everyone's pain and save the family. Martyrs are a cross between hero and scapegoat, sacrificing themselves in an unsuccessful attempt to save the family.

The next two roles, the lost child and the charmer, emerge from feelings of inadequacy. They don't feel good enough to be wanted and think the best way to help the family is by disappearing or becoming invisible.

Charmers, or mascots, entertain the family with their humour and play. Yet underneath they feel as though they are not valued for who they are, but only for what they do to people. Entertaining everyone is, they believe, their best contribution to the family.

All these roles are forms of giving without receiving. A family apportions different jobs to its members in an unsuccessful attempt to find balance and save itself. The more a family is caught up in roles, the more dysfunctional it is; and the more dysfunctional a family is, the more it will get caught in roles. It is a vicious circle.

The truth is a family is a unit. It has a 'group mind', so that at a subconscious level every role and action of family members is a family decision. Every member in the family is co-responsible. From what I have seen in my years of working in therapy, I suggest family dynamics actually generate the subconscious mind.

Unless we are transformed, the family roles are with us for our lifetime. Although we play all the roles in our family, we normally concentrate on one or two in our life. These roles can interfere with forming a relationship. A martyr might be refusing to find a partner because of having to take care of the family or an aged parent. A scapegoat might be so caught up in the role of getting into trouble to save the family that his or her own life may be on hold.

Until you consciously rid yourself of your family role, or you are living at a visionary level, you are caught up in this dynamic. The roles we play become part of our relationships and sooner or later the guilt and sense of failure that led us to play them will surface. If you do not realise that this is a healing process, the beginning of new growth, you will hear these comments as a death knell for your relationship.

Today's Exercise

1 Take a look at your family. Which roles did everyone play?

2 Be willing to make other choices if these roles are not serving you. As you find a new balance, your family will too.

3 Every role is a place where you are off your centre. Ask your Higher Mind to carry you back to your centre, and when you feel a greater sense of peace, ask that your family be carried back to your family's centre.

Don't use your family as an excuse to stay stuck. As you move forward, it will benefit everyone in your family and your life. Family roles and family patterns are among the worst traps to stop you living your purpose and being happy.

Be willing to learn your lessons and not to use anyone or anything to hold yourself back.

No one and nothing is holding me back from having my perfect love.

DAY 20

My Daily Progress Towards My Perfect Mate

....
....
....
....
....
....
....
....
....
....
....
....
....
....
....
....
....

DAY 21

Nothing Is Hard
If You Really Want It

'Nothing is hard if you really want it' is another way of saying commitment opens you up to receive everything you want. I have dealt with this concept a good number of times in hundreds of seminars and workshops. Usually it is fear, guilt, unworthiness, loss or sacrifice which prevents people having what they want. There is always some kind of ambivalence present: if you were not ambivalent you would have your true partner.

From observing the dynamics of thousands of people, one of the core reasons we don't allow ourselves to have it all – love, money, sex, success, etc. – is because we would be embarrassed to win so much and be so successful. We are afraid of having to deal with envy, and so too often we give up on our gifts and talents. We literally make ourselves smaller to fit in with the rest of the crowd.

But having given up our natural gifts, and thus surrendered our leadership qualities and uniqueness, we still want to be special in everyone else's eyes. We become competitive, trying to keep our partners small so we are not threatened by their greatness, and then attacking them if they don't treat us specially enough.

We demand the acknowledgement and attention from others that we are not giving ourselves, or our partners, and so it goes on and on. Every single one of us has fallen into this trap.

Many chapters could be written about specialness. Suffice it to say for now that we mistakenly want our specialness more than we want love. Specialness is a counterfeit love which causes hurt when we are not treated specially enough in the way we want.

If you want something totally, and focus the full power of your mind on it, natural success will follow often in unexpected ways. Using the full power of your mind can open the door to abundance in every area of your life.

My wife, when she was my live-in girlfriend, accurately thought I had a fear of commitment. But at the suggestion of a friend of ours, she decided to 'choose me'.

For three days, she wrestled with her own fear of commitment which had not surfaced before. After burning away the fear, she was ready to commit to me. Paradoxically, simultaneously, as she was choosing me I was caught up in the same process choosing her. We learned the power of really wanting something and choosing it in spite of apparent blocks.

There is a great quotation from Goethe that really speaks of the power of wholly wanting something:

> Until one is committed there is hesitancy.
> The chance to draw back.
> Always ineffectiveness.
> Concerning all acts of initiative (and creation)
> There is one elementary truth.
> The ignorance of which kills countless ideas

and splendid plans:
That the moment one definitely commits
   oneself
Then Providence moves, too.
All sorts of things occur to help one
That would never otherwise have occurred.
A whole stream of events issues from the
   decision
Raising in one's favour
All manner of unforeseen incidents and
   meetings and material assistance,
Which no man would have dreamt would have
   come his way.
Whatever you can do, or dream you can, begin
   it.
Boldness has genius, power, and magic in it.
BEGIN IT NOW.

                              Johann Wolfgang von Goethe

Commitment is the gift of opportunity we give ourselves.

Today's Exercise

Today, let's re-examine ambivalence. Answer the following questions and as answers or thoughts come to you intuitively write them down.

1 What specifically holds you back from having your true partner?

....

2 What style do you have that chases partners away?

....

3 What is it you are afraid of?

....

4 What do you think you would lose if you got a partner?

....

5 What do you feel too guilty about to have your true partner?

....

6 Why don't you deserve your true partner?

....

7 Who would be too jealous of you if you got your perfect partner?

....

Any answer which came up is not the truth! It is a belief you have used against yourself to stop you. You can choose to change them. You can change them with the help of your Higher Mind.

Practise really wanting your perfect mate (not 'needing', but wanting).

If any feelings come up which block this, experience them through until they are complete and a feeling of expectancy is present.

I want my partner more than fear, lack of confidence or anything else that is blocking me.

DAY 21

My Daily Progress Towards My Perfect Mate

DAY 22

Healing Power Struggles

Power struggles are the major stumbling block to an unfolding relationship. If a couple does not learn how to transcend their power struggles, they are unlikely to succeed in their relationship. Many people are afraid of venturing into a committed relationship because they do not think they will survive the fighting, or deadness, caused by competition, which is a subtle form of power struggle.

When I finally decided, at the ripe old age of thirty-six, to commit to one relationship as my best chance for happiness, it was only because I finally felt I had learned and healed enough to have a good chance of success without fighting. If you understand the dynamics of power struggles, you will know what to do to succeed. Awareness is half the battle.

In power struggles, we typically make the biggest mistake in a relationship. We think the other person has been put on earth solely for the purpose of taking care of our needs. We cover this up during the romance stage, but it emerges in force in the power struggle stage, when we fight to have things done our way, which we believe is the 'right way'. We give our partners ultimatums to do it 'my way or take to the highway'. We fight for control. We fight to be the most independent one. We fight to have our needs met first, or twice if our partner is not too tired. A power struggle is a fight to get our partners to meet our needs.

Why we are so afraid to do it our partner's way is because we were hurt, even devastated, as children, when we did it the very way our partner wants us to do it now. We vowed never to do anything like that again so we could not be devastated. For us to do it the way our partner requests can seem like a question of life or death because of the old feelings.

There are a number of ways to resolve this, but one of the easiest is to realise that every competition, every power struggle, is a delaying tactic. It delays the moment when we step forward to resolve the issue and have the needs of both partners healed. In these fights each person looks to the other to fulfil needs which would be best filled by stepping forward.

If you win, if you beat your partner and get your needs met, your partner loses – which means you end up paying the price because as your partner loses, he or she correspondingly become less attractive, which means you lose. If your partner loses, he or she goes into sacrifice, and a level of deadness is introduced into the relationship which again means you are the loser.

If you are not committed to both of you winning 100 per cent, you will find yourself losing to the same extent your partner does. Don't use power struggles as a means to protect the fear that both of you feel, and to keep you both from stepping forward to the next life change. Say 'YES!' to life, so you can move forward easily and fully along with your partner.

Today's Exercise

Think carefully about anyone you are fighting with, or fought with in the past.

What step forward were you afraid of? ....

....

....

What was the gift, or the new level, you turned away from out of fear? ....

....

....

That step, that gift, that new level is still there for you. Be willing to receive this gift or new level for yourself and for all those you love. The step you take is given to your partner through grace.

Who am I fighting with? ....

....

What am I afraid of? ....

....

I deserve the best!

DAY 22

My Daily Progress Towards My Perfect Mate

....

....

....

....

....

....

....

....

....

....

....

....

....

....

....

....

....

Transforming Boredom

Boredom stops relationships! People are afraid of commitment to a relationship for fear of dying a slow and painful death from boredom. *Boredom is easily resolved by taking an emotional risk in communication or intimacy with your partner!* Such risks create new levels of emotional and sexual excitement.

Often when we begin a relationship, we spend the first couple of years, or however long, giving our partners all the gifts we have to give. But at some point the gifts run out, and we feel bankrupt with nothing left to give our partners. In the next phase of the relationship what we can give our partners is our pain. If we give our pain saying 'I give this pain to you so it will no longer come between us', it becomes a major contribution showing confidence in the relationship, and leads to greater intimacy and excitement.

But when we withhold ourselves, usually from fear because we are trying to keep ourselves safe, we end up bored.

The biggest source of boredom in a relationship comes from sacrifice masquerading as love. Everybody has confused sacrifice with love. Sacrifice is counterfeit love. The sacrificer gives, but does not receive. Love is naturally giving and receiving. Giving without receiving leads to 'burn-out' and deadness. Receiving leads to giving at a whole new level.

We go into sacrifice behaviour because we don't value ourselves. At those times when our self-esteem is low we think sacrifice, giving up our own wants and desires, time and money, is the only thing we can offer our partner. It looks to us as if sacrifice, which is a form of self-punishment, is one of the best ways of paying off guilt. So we give ourselves up and use the other's self to carry us forward, but as we do so we lose the points of contact and intimacy which bring excitement and joy to a relationship.

Sacrifice is a form of passive aggression, since withdrawal of contact and withholding is just as deadly as attack. When we complain someone has 'used us', the truth is we used them in order to avoid moving forward.

Sacrifice does not work and bogs down a relationship. It is a form of compromise or adjustment to a situation that needs healing, or resolving, through open and honest communication, otherwise both partners will feel they have lost.

Today's Exercise

1 What communications are you withholding from
   people around you?

I have not told ....

....

....

Be willing to risk sharing those feelings. They are your
feelings. You are responsible for them. They can only
change if you share them intending to heal yourself. If
you try to use them to emotionally control someone into
doing things your way – it won't work!

Sometimes in a relationship, the experiences, thoughts
and feelings you are afraid to share with your partner
because you think they will devastate the other person.
But these are the very things which are killing the relationship because you are withholding them, by
keeping things safe and creating deadness. For instance, if you tell your partner you are no longer
sexually attracted to him or her, it is either the end of
the relationship, or the moment when you accept the
risk and reach for a new level of communication. It is
taking responsibility for feelings of upset and deadness
which must be healed if you, or the relationship, are to
survive. What we withhold are the issues which must
be resolved for our relationships to grow. Sharing these
private and important things and moving past them together can make a relationship exciting again.

2 All sacrifice is based on past and present grievances, against someone you felt did not do it right for you. Your sacrifice is an attempt to show how it should have been done.

List all the sacrifice situations you can remember from when you were a child right up to today so you can discover the hidden grievances.

3 Sacrifice in the present is a way of avoiding what you are frightened to face.

For example:
Sacrifice – I always do things for my boyfriend that I don't want to do or give.

Present grievance – I feel used.

Past grievance – I blame my mother: she always told me I was good when I was doing things for her I didn't want to do.

The trap – I am afraid I have no self-worth because I am afraid to use my creativity.

The excuse it gave me – I used my mother and boyfriend to give me an excuse not to face my creativity.

The solution – communicate, forgive, choose:

> *Communicate:* Let those people know you feel you are in sacrifice to them but take responsibility for it and don't blame them. Remember your sacrifice is a form of using them to hold yourself back.

> *Forgive:* Forgive everyone involved, because forgiveness will heal both of you. Ask for the help

of your Higher Mind and say, 'I forgive [say his or her name], so that we may both be free.'

Choose: Those areas where you feel in role, duty or sacrifice can be turned into pure giving by choosing to give freely rather than doing it because you are supposed to.

DAY 23

My Daily Progress
Towards My Perfect Mate

....

....

....

....

....

....

....

....

....

....

....

....

....

....

....

....

....

DAY 24

Commitment: The Gateway to Freedom

I would like to introduce a notion which single, independent people don't even begin to suspect and which people in committed relationships know: commitment brings freedom generating truth and ease.

Independent people are afraid commitment is a kind of slavery. The spectre of sacrifice is one of the major reasons, ranking alongside heartbreak and jealousy, why people stay single, carefully guarding their independence. Unfortunately, being independent solves nothing – it only hides problems.

We can be independent or inter-dependent. The extent to which we choose independence rather than inter-dependence is the measure of how much we were heartbroken and in sacrifice when we were dependent. It is also the extent to which we are afraid of intimacy.

When we lose our natural bonding in relationships we tend to drop into sacrifice, or fusion, to simulate intimacy. Sometimes the old pain from that sacrifice, or fusion, waits till a new relationship begins and resurfaces to be healed. Bonding, or natural connectedness, cohesiveness and love, nurtures and protects us and by healing the deadness in relationships we can re-enter that natural joyous state.

Commitment brings freedom into existence leading a couple into the truth and ease of real partnership. Miraculously, because a relationship is a team effort and the success of one is enjoyed by both, it only takes one partner to choose commitment to move the couple on to the next step in partnership.

Commitment has the power to shift some of the biggest conflicts in a relationship. Let me explain. Right after the honeymoon or romance stage, we reach the first unpleasant form of power struggle called the shadow stage. This looks like one of the biggest shifts in a relationship. Suddenly our perspective changes and we go from seeing our partner as heaven-sent to being a spectre from hell. Our partner becomes our worst nightmare because we are projecting our greatest fears onto them. We want to get away – to distance ourselves.

This is the moment when we think they have changed for the worst. 'You are not the person I married,' we moan. But the truth is we are punishing them for the problems buried within ourselves, never for theirs. We are punishing them for crimes we feel we have committed.

Commitment does not often spring to mind when we have this negative experience of our partner, but if we re-commit to them at this point, those evil shadows that were scaring us disappear and we step forward into greater partnership having learned the next major lesson about relationships.

Another time when major change seems to occur is when a couple has passed through their power struggles into the Dead Zone. This is a particularly difficult time, full of illusions and pitfalls. Feelings of love and sexual attraction both seem to fall away, and sometimes are replaced with a feeling of revulsion or repulsion towards our partner. Choosing your partner then in that time of darkness paradoxically changes both your experience of them and the relationship itself for the better.

Commitment is prioritising. Because commitment makes your partner more important than your needs and your conflicts, it resolves them. Together with trust, forgiveness and a number of other major healing choices, commitment has the power to shift any problem completely.

Today's Exercise

Today, adopt a new attitude towards commitment because it is what you give in any situation that determines your experience of it. When you give the best of yourself in a relationship you will feel you are the one who is having the best.

Choose a situation, or person, with whom you seem to be in conflict, or where you feel deadness.

I seem to be in conflict with...

....

....

Decide to give 100 per cent to that person or situation and witness the change. You'll know how much you have given by how the relationship enlivens. Our partners never fail unless we stop giving to them.

I choose to commit myself fully to my life by giving myself 100 per cent to the people and the situations that are important to me.

DAY 24

My Daily Progress
Towards My Perfect Mate

....

....

....

....

....

....

....

....

....

....

....

....

....

....

....

....

DAY 25

As You Believe, So Shall It Be

Nothing can happen to you unless you believe it can. Our beliefs make up a matrix which we project out on to the world, which returns looking as if it is what is really happening in the world. If you change your mind, you can literally change the world.

In my work as a therapist and marriage counsellor, I have seen people time and again producing immense change in seemingly impossible situations by applying this principle. When you understand how it works, it's no longer necessary to work at adjusting or changing the outside situation. Instead, you only need find and change the subconscious pattern of belief to accelerate the healing process and put the power of transformation back in your own hands. It gives you the power to get out of one of life's biggest traps: believing that you are a victim.

When I learned this, I experienced some major breakthroughs and insights regarding my own life. The block I had in writing my doctoral dissertation fell away when I correctly identified the subconscious thought that both my parents, who were divorced, would come to my doctoral graduation and somehow get back together again. I realised I was not just writing a dissertation, which was difficult enough, but I was also trying to do the seemingly impossible and bring my family back together. Suddenly I understood why I had nearly died a number of years earlier and what had led me to almost quit life. My near-death experience was subconsciously my last-ditch attempt, by sacrificing myself, to bring my family back together because I felt guilty about what had happened in my family.

Discovering and examining our beliefs is one of the easiest ways to get into our subconscious to change it. In any situation ask yourself intuitively 'What do I believe that could make this happen?' Your intuitive mind is a far better tool for this purpose than your analytical mind because it allows information to pop into your mind. For instance, if your partner has treated you badly, ask yourself 'What must I believe about my partner, relationships and the opposite sex that this could happen?'

Your feelings originate from your beliefs, thoughts, and values. If you believe the opposite sex will reject you, then you are probably overly self-conscious around them because you are afraid of being rejected yet again!

But, here's the bad news, the nature of fear is that whatever you fear you are already feeling. So if you are afraid of rejection, you are feeling rejected. When you feel rejected, you act rejected and that leads to rejectable behaviour.

Repeatedly I observe several common types of behaviour resulting from this belief: trying too hard, running away, or acting as if it doesn't matter. Usually this causes us to encounter the exact feeling we are most afraid of, which reinforces the belief and keeps us locked into a vicious circle.

Thousands of times I have discovered the same core belief, blocking people from finding partners or allowing their relationships to work – the thought that they were not wanted by either their mother or father.

This belief is quite easy to shift. Once I had worked through it myself, I discovered I could help others move through it in less than an hour.

I once worked with a woman whose mother had tried to abort her with darning needles. When that didn't work, she jumped off chairs and drank toxic substances. Needless to say, mother and daughter had been in power struggles since before the birth, which had made the birth experience traumatic for both of them. The mother would shout at her daughter that she hated, and had never wanted, her. This was a deeply entrenched, well-established behaviour pattern, but we were able to clear it up in less than an hour with a great deal of laughter, which is sometimes as healing as tears.

We started by establishing that many of the things her mother said were a result of the extreme power struggle they were both in. My client, the daughter, could understand this because she, too, said things she didn't mean in the heat of anger.

My client soon realised, with a good deal of humour, that in their war her score was far higher. She remembered with relish the dirty tricks she had successfully played on her mother, like screaming so loudly that everyone in the village knew her mother was punishing her even to the extent that sometimes the village priest would come running to rescue her.

It was easy to take my client back intuitively to the time when the abortion attempts first began. The mother had just received word that her husband had been killed in the war. She had no money.

I asked my client, as hard as it might be considering the truth of the circumstances, to imagine her mother at that time as confident, resourceful and abundant. When my client had that picture, I asked her how her mother felt about her pregnancy, given she had those qualities. My client smiled and said her mother really wanted her now.

Next, I asked my client to consider which was true, whether her mother hadn't wanted her personally, or whether it was pain, lack of confidence, and fear that had caused her mother's actions. Obviously it had not been personal. So I asked her, now she realised her mother wasn't personally rejecting her, if in truth she had been the one rejecting her mother all along. With a smile as big as the room, the woman admitted she had been rejecting her mother and making life hell for her.

I asked her why, what was her purpose in believing she was rejected by her mother. She replied this gave her, from her earliest years, the permission to be independent and do whatever she wanted. By the way, I find this is often the purpose of early trauma. Now through her new understanding she could forgive her mother and experience a whole new level of self-worth, desirability, inclusion, fun, confidence and peace. Immediately her relationship with her mother took a giant step forward and her mother seemed completely different the next time they talked. This woman was not the most difficult client I've ever worked with in this type of trauma, but she was one of the more dramatic.

Be comforted; anyone with any willingness at all can move successfully through deeply held beliefs like this into fulfilling and happy relationships.

Today's Exercise

Today, consider your relationship situation.

List the beliefs you must have had for the situation to be the way it is: ....

....

....

....

....

If you don't like the situation or the beliefs, make a choice which will serve you better. Beliefs can easily be changed. As soon as you realise you have them, make another choice about them.

I am making new choices...

....

DAY 25

My Daily Progress Towards My Perfect Mate

Do You Want Your Relationship or Your Story?

Your personality has been putting together your life story for years. Typically, it is filled with painful and heroic episodes all neatly tied together to prove what a good person you are.

Anything you try hard to prove means you believe the opposite. If I were to attempt to convince you how bright I am, pretty soon you would begin to suspect that either I was insecure about my intelligence or that I was unintelligent. Our stories or concepts about ourselves are the most primordial aspects of ourselves that limit joy and generate all our victim patterns and problems with our families and other relationships.

Let us look at some of the underlying concepts in our stories.

One way we tell our story is: 'I am the way I am because this has been done to me by others.' A more honest statement, if we were truly aware of our subconscious motivation, would be: 'I used others – I had them do things to me so I wouldn't have to face my fears of the next step, and so I'd have an excuse to do things my way.'

That statement has been one of the fundamental

dynamics in thousands of people with whom I've worked who were molested. Most of them were precocious sexually even as children. Being afraid of what they would grow into if they continued on their path of sexual precocity, they created trauma which then blocked them. That way they could satisfy their curiosity without responsibility. While not the only dynamic in molestation, this is the most common in those people with whom I've worked at a subconscious level.

Our life stories are largely composites of victim and martyr stories. Suffering is a veiled form of attack and so this is a way of feigning innocence while attacking. This is not an easy area to explore because typically we keep it all hidden from our conscious mind. Our story is all consuming. We are the heroes and heroines, but the problem is that the natural reward for all our good, or heroic actions, does not go to us: it goes to our story. It is the movie of our life.

In our movies we are the stars, the directors, producers, script writers and cameramen, and we make everyone else our supporting actors and actresses. But everybody else is doing the same thing. So we get into trouble in our relationships because we have been cast as the supporting roles in their movies.

Many people script their movies as epic tragedies. It takes effort and understanding to transcend our personal stories. First we must turn our stories into happy stories which is a great challenge for most of us. After years of working with people to clear away tens of thousands of behavioural and emotional patterns and to shift the accumulated debris of hundreds of thousands of problems, I've learned I must focus on the story that people are writing, and assist them to see the payoffs they are getting are definitely not worth it.

Today's Exercise

Begin to examine your story, the one you are writing in your life, especially where it covers relationships.

Take ten minutes to write at least a page about your relationship story or tell it to a friend or dictate it to a tape recorder.

My story: ....

....

....

....

....

....

....

....

....

Pick out the key patterns which repeat again and again or which run through your story.

My key patterns are ....

....

....

What are you trying to prove by your story? ....

....

....

What is the purpose of having this type of story?

....

....

If you don't like what you've found, make some new decisions about what you want.

No matter how good your story, you deserve better.

I am turning my story over to my Higher Mind.

DAY 26

My Daily Progress
Towards My Perfect Mate

DAY 27

Grace of Intimacy

One of our great fears in life is the fear of intimacy. Intimacy is joining with someone – moving through all your blocks, considerations, and fears to a heartfelt closeness.

When we get right down to the bottom line there are only two feelings, love and fear.

Love is the root of very positive emotion. Love underlies joy and happiness, while fear is at the bottom of every negative emotion like anger, hatred or depression.

Years ago, my wife and I discovered that our blocks and problems were in those places where we had not yet connected in intimacy. As we did so, the problems between us, and around us, disappeared. We started to apply this powerful lesson to the problems of our family and friends with excellent results.

Let's consider the problem of infidelity in terms of intimacy and the subconscious mind. There are three core, subconscious dynamics round infidelity for both parties.

1 Fear – both parties are afraid of intimacy. The infidelity becomes a good excuse to avoid becoming more

intimate, to prevent the partner meaning too much, or to end the relationship.

2   Power struggle – which is another form of fear. This kind of struggle can be a method used by the 'victimised' partner to become independent, or the one having an affair to get revenge or gain control.

3   A lack of bonding and fulfilment which leads to fantasy, emptiness and finally infidelity.

Intimacy, which is love made manifest, has the power and grace to heal all problems because one of the core aspects to unlocking any problem is that there is always separation present. For instance, when we fall ill there is a part of us which feels cut off and unloved. If we can find and integrate that part, the illness disappears. The power of intimacy and love allows a grace which transforms problems easily to become manifest.

Intimacy seems to be everything we ever wanted, but we are afraid of our own sense of inadequacy and unworthiness, or we are afraid we will lose ourselves if we join with another.

Intimacy is not romance, which is based on our dreams about the other; it is a real sharing of heart, mind and energy in such a way that we move forward confidently. When we are prepared to take the next step in intimacy it has the same effect as saying 'yes' to life. We move forward; we grow.

One technique which makes intimacy more possible is simply being with, or moving towards your partner without judgement, until you feel mutuality and 'joining'. When you join your partner with love, problems and their symptoms seem to disappear and a new grace and confidence appears.

I have found the intimacy of 'joining' to be effective in

healing. If I have a problem and my partner does not, or if my partner has a problem and I do not, or if we both have a problem, our 'joining' each other shifts the problem to a new level of experience.

As problem after problem emerges and is healed in your relationship, your enjoyment and ability to give and receive will grow. By awareness and practice you will begin to notice separation as it emerges so that you can join your partner in a new level of loving and intimacy.

Today's Exercise

Today, find someone to 'join' with in order to help that person, to help yourself, or to help you both. Don't stop until you feel the release that intimacy brings.

Keep moving towards them until you join them and feel joy and peace.

Practise this as often as you can, for it will empower you to move forward in your relationship whatever the nature of the problem.

I joined with ....

....

I experienced ....

....

I learned ....

....

....

DAY 27

My Daily Progress Towards My Perfect Mate

....
....
....
....
....
....
....
....
....
....
....
....
....
....
....
....
....

DAY 28

Feel the Joy

Most people think that first you find a partner and then you feel joyful. Actually, it works the other way round. Your partner comes along because a level of energy and joy, which is hugely attractive, begins to well up inside you and attracts your perfect mate.

The more you feel joy, the more beautiful you become. Just like when spring arrives and all the flowers begin to bloom, so naturally the bees appear.

So much would just come to us if we chose joy first and let that be a part of our lives. If you are joyful, you have already achieved the purpose of a relationship.

Joy is a choice we can make all the time instead of choosing our stories. It is a choice for love instead of fear. At a subconscious level, every problem we have has the purpose of causing something to happen that will bring us joy. But some choices we make are grave mistakes bringing us many things other than happiness.

If you think it is your partner's job to make you happy, you are placing inordinate pressure on the other person. Your partner can never succeed at *making* you happy because of the nature of expectations and demands. Make no demands, have no expectations. Instead, give all you can and love all you can, especially in those areas where you want things from your partner because that will create joy and receiving in your relationship. Your joy is the best gift you can give your partner. It is irresistible.

Today's Exercise

Today, if you experience anything other than joy, say to yourself: 'I could be feeling joy instead of this.'

At the beginning of the day, and at every hour, choose joy. If you find yourself caught in something you don't like:

1 Admit you don't want it.

2 Recognise it is not ultimate truth, because it is not joy.

3 Let go of any hidden payoffs which you gain from the bad feelings.

4 Turn it over to your Higher Mind, and once again choose joy.

This is the best gift you can give to your partner, your parents, your children, the world, and God. Anything else is really just a form of revenge.

I am choosing to have joy in every moment of my life!

DAY 28

My Daily Progress Towards My Perfect Mate

DAY 29

Temptations – Accept No Substitute

For a number of years I have noticed women coming to my seminars hoping to find a partner. Often they blossomed in joy, but the next time I visited their country they were dejected and depleted once more. Some time ago I decided to take a closer look at what was going on.

I found out that they had found the perfect mate within a fortnight, except for one thing – he was married or in another relationship. Was it coincidence, or bad karma, or was something else afoot? Within six months I had the answer.

When you are wide open in joy, the personality doesn't have much to stop you with, so it offers you a last trap. Along comes a *simulated* Mr or Ms 100 per cent perfect. They are really Mr or Ms 85 per cent perfect because they are in another relationship. But, because he, or she, has not had someone to love and be loved by for a long time, the temptation is seemingly irresistible and they fall into the trap of a triangular relationship. This is a horrible trap which causes guilt and delays happiness.

The usual scenario is that the person who is wide

open chooses Mr or Ms 85 per cent and completely misses Mr or Ms 100 per cent because they are deeply involved in the triangular relationship. Sometimes they notice the 100 per cent possibilities but miss their importance because they are already lured into the trap.

Now, when I see women leaving a workshop in that starry-eyed way, I give them my best advice: if they meet Mr 85 per cent, I say enjoy the connection and friendship, but don't get involved romantically because Mr 100 per cent is waiting in the wings, he's on his way. It is important not to settle for less. If they follow my advice, they will have a new friend and before long a lover. Don't settle for less.

Accept no substitutes! Everyone wins bigger, if you win bigger. Stay open to having it all. It's what you deserve.

Today's Exercise

Today, affirm you can have a 100 per cent relationship. Enjoy your new connections.

Trust yourself and trust the process.

If you stand empty handed with trust and joy, your attractiveness only grows. If a Mr/Ms 85 per cent shows up, it's usually an indication that Mr/Ms 100 per cent is close behind.

I can have my 100 per cent perfect relationship.

DAY 29

My Daily Progress
Towards My Perfect Mate

The Path of Relationships

The path of relationships is the quickest path of growth. Through the healing path of relationships, growth that would take hundreds of years of fighting temptations or decades of meditation can be accomplished in a much shorter time frame.

Everything between you and your wholeness, the realisation of oneness, will come up in your relationship. Every bit of unfinished business with family members, old loves, friends, etc. *will come up disguised as problems in the here and now of relationships.*

Actually, this is the good news because it is these blocks inside us that stop us. So even though this old pain in new forms is uncomfortable to confront, if you face it with the right attitude it becomes a way to heal and move forward time and again. Once you commit yourself to your partner and love him or her more than your own story, your love can stop time and start eternity.

The support of a loving relationship allows you to face the deepest layers of pain successfully and if you adopt the right attitude you will soon recognise the process is healing and helping you mature. And you will swiftly learn your partner is not your enemy.

Once you give up your need to be special, you can have love and learn to be harmless in a way that provides true safety and allows a 'joining' which makes miracles possible. Once you stop attacking your partner because of your or his or her needs, or blaming your partner for what you are doing (which is what we always do), then you have the possibility of leaping forward, sweeping blocks aside and finding solutions in a time-transcending way.

A relationship teaches you to receive, which is crucial to your own personal growth and to be a partner, which is crucial for your mental, emotional and spiritual growth.

As you partner with your mate, you learn to partner with your Higher Mind and to allow the power of grace to come into your life, rather than having to 'do' everything yourself. 'Doing it' yourself locks you into a kind of independence which makes any relationship a fight or struggle. 'Doing it' yourself means it may or may not get done. But 'doing it' with the grace of the Higher Mind means it will be accomplished easily.

The truth is it is easy to find your perfect mate but much harder to keep him or her! Finding your perfect mate is the beginning of a great adventure in love and consciousness.

Decide now that you are going to find – *and* keep – your perfect mate.

Decide now that you will learn all the lessons you need to learn to keep the relationship unfolding gracefully.

Decide now to become an expert on those things that

support life and love: intimacy, communication, forgiveness, trust, giving and receiving, commitment, and letting go.

Choose to commit with your partner to realise your wholeness rather than making your relationship the battleground of specialness and needs.

Choose now to develop a relationship with your Higher Mind, for that will naturally lead you into openness, partnership and living a life of grace.

Today's Exercise

Focus on becoming an expert on the path of relationships so your love will create miracles.

Choose the path of relationships to accelerate your own healing and growth.

Intend that your perfect partner comes to you as part of your healing path.

The great adventure has just begun. May you choose to have smooth sailing. And may your story be a happy one!

I intend to find and keep my perfect mate in a loving and fulfilling life!

DAY 30

My Daily Progress
Towards My Perfect Mate

Additional

Exercises

Do these additional exercises *one week* after you have finished the workbook:

Pick the two lessons which stand out as the most important for you and review them a day at a time. On the third day, put the numbers one to thirty in a bowl. Pick five numbers and review the five lessons one a day, for five days.

Do the following exercises *one month* after you have finished the workbook:

Firstly, repeat the same procedure with five numbers picked from the bowl and review those lessons.

Then answer these questions:

What is it I really want? ....

....

What is it I keep choosing? ....

....

If you haven't got what you want, now is the time to choose again.

You can give yourself what you want.

You can have what you want.

You deserve a perfect mate. He or she has been experiencing events very much like those you have gone through in your life, in a pretty similar way. The story was different, but the experiences and feelings were similar. If you lose hope, it will mean your perfect mate will also lose hope.

What do you really want? All it takes is willingness . . . and love.

Afterword

This is a section to be read *one week and one month* after you have finished your thirty-day course. It is a way of re-examining where you are and how you feel about the process of finding your perfect mate.

First of all, ask yourself honestly and intuitively what percentage, on the scale of 100 per cent, you actually feel open to finding your perfect mate.

If the answer is anything less than 100 per cent, ask yourself these questions and write down your responses.

1 What do I value more than my perfect mate?

2 What holds me back from my perfect mate?

3 What am I afraid I will lose if I get my perfect mate?

4 What have I not forgiven from the past that holds me back?

5 Is there anything I don't do or do which stops my

partner coming to me? Is there anything in my attitude which would chase me away if I met myself as a prospective partner? Whatever that is – let it go.

6 Is there anything I can think of that I or my perfect mate 'has to do' to have a partner? Every time we say 'have to', 'should', 'got to', 'need to', 'ought to', or 'must', we create resistance even to what we say we want. Choosing instead of expecting opens up possibilities.

What is my attitude to having my perfect mate? What am I expecting? ....

....

No matter what you are experiencing, you can choose to have your perfect mate. Whatever you are experiencing, whatever your attitude, choose to have your perfect mate now, unless you value something else more. Remember, if we waited till we were 100 per cent ready for a relationship, most of us wouldn't have one.

If you would like to continued exploring the principles outlined in *30 Days to Find Your Perfect Mate*, you can obtain more information from the following address:

Psychology of Vision Centre
PO Box 7
Leatherhead
Surrey
KT23 4YF

Phone 0372-451 979